Finding Out With Your SENSES

We use our senses all of the time. We smell, touch, see, and hear the world around us. We enjoy the taste of food. We hear our friends laughing or leaves rustling. We notice people grin or frown. We smell the spring rain and new flowers.

FINDING OUT WITH YOUR SENSES presents very simple experiments for children. The author poses questions and suggests projects for the readers. Children will learn about different aspects of their senses. For example, they will learn that we actually "taste" some food more with our noses than with our tongues. They will enjoy looking at the world through colored cellophane, touching fur and wool in the dark, and doing other projects. They will love the opportunity to do things by themselves, experimenting and thereby learning new concepts about the world and their own bodies.

Lively, large, enjoyable illustrations accompany the text. They will help the readers visualize the projects, so that they may carry them out with greater success.

Also By Seymour Simon:
LET'S TRY IT OUT . . . WET & DRY
LET'S TRY IT OUT . . . LIGHT & DARK
DISCOVERING WHAT EARTHWORMS DO
DISCOVERING WHAT FROGS DO
DISCOVERING WHAT GOLDFISH DO

And For Older Readers:
ANIMALS IN FIELD AND LABORATORY

Finding Out
With Your SENSES

By Seymour Simon

Illustrated by
Emily McCully

McGRAW-HILL
BOOK COMPANY

New York • St. Louis • San Francisco • Dusseldorf • Johannesburg
Kuala Lumpur • London • Mexico • Montreal • New Delhi • Panama
Rio de Janeiro • Singapore • Sydney • Toronto

For Michael, the founder of the Penguin Club

Library of Congress Catalog Number: 72-136186

ISBN 07-057430-8
234567890 HDEC 75432

Every day is an exploring day for you.
Look at a high-flying kite and
cloud shapes in the sky.
Listen to your friends at play and
fire engines going by.
Stroke a cat's smooth fur and
a rough tree trunk.
Smell what someone is cooking for dinner.
Taste a sour pickle and
a stick of peppermint gum.

You can find out about so many things
by seeing,
    hearing,
        touching,
            smelling,
                tasting—
by using all your senses.
Each day there's something different
for you to see and to hear.

Each day brings new things to touch,
to taste, and to smell.
Where do you find new things to explore
with your senses?
They are in your room, in the kitchen,
out-of-doors, all around you.

Seeing is one way of finding out.
You can tell how large things are
by looking at them.
Is the building bigger than the tree?
Which of your friends is the tallest?
You can also tell the shape of things
by looking at them.

What is the shape of a wheel, a ball,
or a tin can?
Can you or your friends tell the kind
of a car by its shape?
Can you tell the difference between a boy's
bike and a girl's bike by the way they look?

Sometimes it's not easy to tell the size
or shape of an object.
From the ground, an airplane flying
high above looks very tiny.
From an airplane, people walking
on the streets below look as small as ants.

How big does the moon look to you?
Look at the close-up photos of the moon
taken by the astronauts.
You can see that the moon is really a
large object.
The further away an object is from you,
the smaller it looks.
From where you are on the earth,
you can block out the sight of the moon
with your small thumb.
Try it out.

Try to catch a rubber ball thrown high in the air.
Now close one eye and try to catch it again.

Watch out!

It's much harder to catch a ball using only one eye.
Close one eye again and try to bring your two index
fingers together tip to tip.
Now try it with both eyes open.
Using two eyes helps us to see how near or far things are.

What else can you find out by looking?
Look at a yellow pencil, a red fire engine,
and a green leaf.
You can see many different colors around you.
Mix paints of different colors to see what new
colors you can make.
Mix blue and yellow paint to get green.
Mix red and blue to get purple.
Try your own mixtures and see what you get.

Sunlight looks white, but it really is made
of many different colors.
You can see the colors that make up white light
when you see a rainbow.
The colors are called the spectrum.
They are always arranged in the same order,
red, orange, yellow, green, blue, and violet.
The edge of a mirror or a glass prism in sunlight
shining on a white paper shows a spectrum.

You can find out about the size, the distance,
the shape, and the color of objects by looking at them.
You can find out other things about objects
even when you cannot see them.
Close your eyes and listen.
There are sounds all around you.
Can you tell the difference between the
sounds you hear?
Listen to the rumble of a truck and
the voices of your friends at play.
Listen to the sound of footsteps
and the barking of a dog.

You have to listen carefully
for quieter sounds.
Listen to the sound of the wind
or the sound of falling rain.

19

Try to make different kinds of sounds
with different objects.
Walk on dried leaves and listen to them crackle.
Shake a pebble in a can and make it rattle.
Snap your fingers, clap your hands,
make different sounds with your mouth.

Lightly tap a tall thin drinking glass
with a spoon.
Add a little water to the glass
and tap it again.
How does the sound change?

Take two pencils and stretch
a rubber band between them.
Twang the rubber band with your finger.
Stretch the rubber band further apart and
twang it again.

How are the twangs different?
You can find out about lots of things by
listening carefully.

How can you tell the difference between
different cloths that look alike?
Touch a piece of wool, a piece of cotton,
and a piece of nylon.
Do they feel different?
You can use any part of your body to touch things,
but you usually use your fingers to find out
how things feel.

Put a bunch of things in a shoe box:
marbles, cotton balls, rocks, nails,
rubber bands, pencils, chalk, fur,
pieces of metal, and so on.
Cover your eyes and put your hand in the box.
Just by touching, try to tell what each object is.

Let a friend try.
Ask him to tell you how each object feels.
He may say that an object feels rough or smooth,
light or heavy, round or long, flat or thick.
He may also say that an object feels
cold or warm, or even wet or dry.
Your sense of touch tells you many things.
Try it out.

You taste with your tongue and smell
with your nose.
Some tastes are easy to tell about.
Taste a piece of sugar.
Rinse out your mouth and taste a slice of lemon.

Rinse again and taste a salty peanut.
Rinse again and taste a drop of black coffee.
Sweet, sour, salty, and bitter are easy
tastes to tell.
But many foods have more than one of these
different tastes.
They may be sweet and sour or any other mixture.

Some odors are pleasant to smell.
You may like the smell of flowers, or of
perfume, or of a hamburger sizzling on a grill.

Other odors are not very nice: a car's exhaust,
rotting food, or burning rubber.
Some odors are easy to tell: ammonia, vinegar,
or an angry skunk.

Other odors are more difficult to tell: the seashore,

the pages of a new book,

chalk dust on a blackboard.

Taste and smell are two senses that are
sometimes mixed up with each other.
When you say, that a piece of apple pie
is delicious, you probably mean
that it both tastes and smells good.
Try this with a friend.
Blindfold him with a handkerchief.
Tell him that you are going to give him
certain foods to taste and that he is to
try to tell you what they are.
Give him a slice of apple to taste,
and at the same time hold a slice of onion
under his nose.
He probably will say that he is eating an onion.

Now ask him to hold his nose and give him a
slice of onion to taste.
He will have a hard time telling what it is
without being able to smell it.
It's often difficult to tell the taste of foods
without also smelling them.

Look, listen, touch, smell, and taste.
Use all your senses to explore the world
around you.

39

ABOUT THE AUTHOR

SEYMOUR SIMON has been a science teacher for the last twelve years. He is a science book reviewer, has served as a science consultant, and has had over fifty articles published by Scholastic Publications. He has also written juvenile science books, including *ANIMALS IN THE FIELD AND LABORATORY, DISCOVERING WHAT EARTHWORMS DO, DISCOVERING WHAT GOLDFISH DO, WET AND DRY,* and *LIGHT AND DARK.* A native New Yorker, he has done graduate work in psychology and biology. Mr. Simon lives in Great Neck, New York, with his wife and two boys.

ABOUT THE ARTIST

EMILY ARNOLD McCULLY was born in Galesburg, Illinois. She received her A.B. degree from Brown University and her M.A. in Art History from Columbia University. She has done many illustrations for magazines, book jackets, and children's books. Mrs. McCully lives in Swarthmore, Pennsylvania with her husband, who is a professor of history at Swarthmore College.